CLEVELAND RADIO PLAYERS

Published by Cleveland Radio Players

Copyright © 2015 by Milton Matthew Horowitz

All rights, including the right of reproduction in whole or in part, in any form, including digital reproduction, are reserved. Published in the United States by Cleveland Radio Players.

CAUTION: Professionals and amateurs are hereby warned that *Manderella*, being fully protected under the Copyright Laws of the United States is subject to royalty. All rights, including professional, amateur, motion picture, recitation, lecturing, public reading, radio and television broadcasting, and the rights of translation into foreign languages, are strictly reserved. Particular emphasis is laid on the question of readings, permission for which must be secured in writing from the author's representative at Cleveland Radio Players, 2218 Superior Ave, Suite 203, Cleveland, OH 44114. The amateur acting rights of *Manderella* are controlled exclusively for the author by the author's representative.

ISBN-13: 978-0692357590 (Cleveland Radio Players, The)

Original adaption and Performances

Originally adapted for the radio and performed by The Cleveland Radio Players. Directed by Milton Matthew Horowitz. Recorded at Bad Racket Studios.

Starring:

Denny Castiglione	Narrator
Charles Hargrave	Manderella
Cory Shy	Bro 1
David Flynt	Bro 2
Michael Lawrence	Bro 3
Kat Bi	Princess
Jack Matuszewski	Duke of Tubonia
Jack Hunt	Jonah
Eric Sever	Fairy Godfather
Beau Reinker	Stepfather
	Older Gentleman
	Little Boy
	Guy on Toilet

Manderella A Very Fairy Tale

By

Milton Matthew Horowitz

The Cleveland Radio Players
2218 Superior Ave #203
Cleveland Ohio 44114

www.clevelandradioplayers.com
theradioplayers@gmail.com
216 269 4171

MANDERELLA

the stage should be set with 3 homeless looking guys gathered around trash cans scrummaging for scraps and trying to keep warm. The narrator may be on or off stage dictating the action of the play through the entire play by simply reading the stage action aloud. for this reason all the lighting direction has been left absent. the narrator may also be used to bookend the film by just speaking at the beginning and the end of the play.

cast

MEN

> NARRATOR
> (optional)
> may be on or off stage... directors choice

> MANDERELLA
> the male love interest of the princess. Manderella is fraigle and sweet

> THE FAIRY GODFATER
> (FGF)
> The Fairy Godfather is manderellas creepy gaurdian angle who has only just begun to watch over him

> BROTHER 1
> (Bro 1)
> the youngest and meanest of manderellas brother

> BROTHER 2
> (Bro 2)
> the middle child, equally as hateful as brother 1 but only half as smart. he mindlessly follows whatever his younger brother says

> BROTHER 3
> (bro 3)
> the eldest of the three brothers who rarely talks

> WICKED STEP FATHER
> manderellas step father who rarely speaks execpt to yell at manderella, can be played on stage with doubling by the Duke or the

> **WICKED STEP FATHER**
> princess or anyone else as mearly
> an arm in a chair with its back to
> the audience

> **THE DUKE OF TUBONIA**
> what would usually be known as a
> king is instead known as the Duke
> of Tubonia. The Duke is large and
> in charge and totes a tube around
> him at all times

> **JONAH**
> Jonah is a faithful scribe who
> takes great pride in his duty to
> the Duke

> **THE ROYAL SHOE FITTER**
> a man of little words but big
> apearance... like that of a secret
> service agent with mirror finish
> aviators.

WOMEN

> **THE PRINCESS**
> the princess should be juxed
> opposed to Manderella... if
> manderella is tall and slender and
> white... then the princess is short
> and thick ...and black perhaps...
> or vice versa

> **THE NARRATOR**
> (optional)
> the narrator again may be on or off
> stage and played by either a male
> or female directors choice.

ACT I

SCENE 1

THE GARBAGE ALLEY

> (the stage should be set with
> 3 homeless looking guys
> gathered around trash cans
> scrummaging for scraps and
> trying to keep warm.)

> **NARRATOR**
> nevemind those homeless guys
> rummaging through the trash...

                    NARRATOR
they're story is ... well...the
story I'm about to tell you... the
begining of there is about a man...
no... wait... it's about a boy...
no that s not right... it's about
a man-boy... yeah that's it... he's
a man-boy...and this man-boy's
story begins in a shitty house on
the poor side of town. A lonely
man-boy who wanted nothing more
then to meet a beautiful princess
that would take him away from his
wretched life...ya see this lonley
man boy lived with his 3 evil step
brothers and his evil step
Father... his real father died in a
horrible peanut related alergic
reation... he never really met his
father but a crude painting made a
passing gypsy was created in his
fathers likeness was left behind to
him from his late mother... his
mother died years latter in a
terrible balogny feeding racoon
incident when she contracted rabies
from a rabbid racoon and had to be
put down... now all that remanind
of the man boys parents was the
crude painting and the crumbling
house...oh and his name...didn't I
tell you... His name was
Manderella... and with his name
came a great blessing he never knew
about until one very certain day
where his fabulous secret would be
reveald to him... so let us watch
and laugh in amusment at our
Manderella...

THE ATTIC

In the attic of this crumby house is young Manderella. He is
a young skinny lad with brown hair and raggedy clothes. He
is whistling a happy tune and sewing with a needle and
thread.

Manderella pulls out a painting of a beach and sighs.

                                            MANDERELLA SIGHS

>   MANDERELLA
> Low...How wretched am I. How I wish
> to one day marry a lady who will
> take me away from this crumby
> place. Oh who do I kid, I am just a
> ..just a...dirty... man... boy ...
> servant. Not a soul would dare to
> fall in love with low class dirty
> servant like me.

SFX: AIR HORN

3 BROTHERS YELLING

>   ALL THREE BOTHERS
> Hay Manderella!... hay up there

>   MANDERELLA
> They can make me do their crumby
> chores, but they cant stop me from
> dreaming ....ain't that
> right dad?

Manderella glances over at a Painting of his father on the wall as if it were going to reply... but it does not... his brothers continue to yell

>   ALL THREE BOTHERS
> Hay Manderella!... get down here!

Manderella covers the painting and then heads downstairs to the kitchen

the three brothers are sitting at a table eating peanuts and throwing the discarded shells on the floor at Manderelas feet. Manderella walks in the kitchen.

>   BROTHER 1
> Hey..what a..what are all these
> peanuts doin on the floor here?

>   MANDERELLA
> Well I uhh-

>   BROTHER 1
> CLEAN IT UP!

>   BROTHER 2
> Yeah ...(laughing)... Clean it up

                    BROTHER 3
                 (laughs and snorts)

Mandarella walks over to his brother to grab the broom, when
his suddenly grabs him by the arm

                                          BROTHER 1 SNIFFING

             BRO 1
        You smell rank stinker-Ella! you
        need to take a bath!

             BRO 2
        Yeah ... Stink-a-rella ...cause he
        stinks!

as bully-some as Manderellas two step brothers are they dare
not laugh at something their eldest brother does not find
funny...

                                                   SILENCE

             BROTHER 3
        Hahahahahah ....

but once he begins to laugh...

                                            3 BROTHERS LAUGH

                    MANDERELLA
        Yeah fellas I'll freshen up right
        after I tidy up a bit.

             BRO 1
        Fuck(Hell)yeah you will!

All 3 of Manderellas brothers shove him as they walk by and
exit the kitchen, leaving Mandarella to sweep up the very
thing that killed his father... upon finishing sweeping up
the peanuts Manderella quickly hurrys to bathroom to take a
bath

THE BATHROOM

Manderella turns on the shower and the dirtiest water begins
to comes out of faucet.

                                       CUE RUNNING WATTER SOUND

Manderella is use to the dirty water so he turns to the
mirror and begins to talk to himself.

                    MANDERELLA
          Im gonna have a good day today I
          can feel it!...Its in the air
          tonight.

                                        CUE PHILL COLLINS ESK MUSIC

The tub now full of dirty water is ready for Manderellas
bath

                                        CUE MOUSE SOUNDS

but before he can dip a toe in the tub he notices three mice
struggle to swim about in it. Unphased by the vermin
Manderella attempts to make new friends out of this very
gross situation

                    MANDERELLA
          Well how do you like that ....Worry
          not my filthy vermin friends...I
          shall be thy savior...
          Suppose ill just ...scoop you
          fellas up.

Manderella scoops his new found mice friends into a bucket
then eagerly sits in the water, lays back, and lights a
candle. He then closes his eye and tries to relax for a
moment when suddenly.

                                        LOUD KNOCK AT THE DOOR

                    BRO 1
          HAY!....Pop says go feed those
          raccoons on the roof ... they were
          scratchin noise all night.

one brother throws two handfuls of bologna into tub at
Manderelss and the other Brother assaults him by throwing a
handful of peanuts into tub. The eldest brother looks on in
approval

                    BRO 3
          Nice...Nice...good work little
          brothers...

                                        ALL 3 BROTHERS LAUGHING AND EXIT

                    MANDERELLA
          -sigh-

The brothers exit finally giving Manderella peace after
ruining his dirty bath water with bologna and peanut
crumbs... Knowing his brothers will only bully him worse if

he doesn't do what they ask ... he hurry's up his bath and places his newly found mice friends safely in his attic room away from his brother before heading out to feed the racoons.

SIDE OF THE HOUSE

Manderellas house is falling apart... mainly do to the fact that a family of racoons live on the roof and inside the walls of the crumbling home...

                              RACCOON CHATTER

forced to feed the very critters that killed his mother by his wicked step father ... toting a bucket full of bologna he says

                    MANDERELLA
          well...I Suppose I oughta do this
          now....

                          MORE RACCOON CHATTER

Manderella begins to toss the bologna like a Frisbee onto the roof... tiny little meat Frisbees fly onto the roof as the raccoons scurry out to eat them when suddenly, Manderellas brother appear on the balcony of the home...

                    BRO 1
          Hey fag-a-rella! ...we got some
          Laundry for ya.

His brothers begin to toss heaping loads of laundry at him and all around him

                    BRO 2
          Yeah throw laundry at
          him...(laughing)

Humilated Manderella begins to emerge from the mountian of laundry

                    BRO 1
          Fuckin get it done... and when your
          finished with that... pops want his
          coffee.

                    BRO 2
          Yeah... and make sure it's hot this
          time god dammit

laughing, the three brothers exit the balcony but not before the eldest brother lifts his middle finger, flicking Mandarella off as he strolls back inside the house.

                    MANDERELLA
          Right guys ill just .... get right
          on that.

Manderella looks down at laundry everywhere and sighs.

                                        MANDERELLA SIGHS

He knows he doesn't have much of a choice so her hurry's up
as fast as he can to avoid any further harassment from his
brothers... he spends hours cleaning and folding and
cleaning and folding... and just when hes about finished,
Manderella emerges from the basement whistling with a
freshly folded basket of laundry.

PART 2

THE LIVING ROOM

                                        MANDERELLA WHISTELING

his Brothers hear Manderella coming up stairs. and One
brother trips Manderella as he enters...

                                        THUD AND TUMBLEING

Manderella falls spilling all of the freshly folded laundry
to the floor. His other brother joins in by throwing an
empty beer can at his head.

                                        BEER CAN CLINK AND CLANK

                                        BROTHERS LAUGHING

All of the sudden the faint sound of a tuba can be heard in
the distance

                                        FAINT TUBA PLAYING

                    BRO 1
          Hay... do you hear that?

                    BRO 2
          yeah I think I do...

                    BRO 1
          What is that?

                    MANDERELLA
          It sounds like a Tuba

                    BRO 2
            Shut up

                    BRO 1
            Yeah Shut up Manderella you don't
            know anything

there faint sound in the background is indeed the sounds of
a tuba...ya see on the other side of town on top of the hill
lived THE DUKE OF TUBONIA. The Duke was pretty kick ass and
played a Tuba everywhere he went... only problem was ...
nobody knew who he was or how he came to rule over everyone
in town... never the less nobody dare question it... it
would seem as if this is just how things are

THE DUKES PALACE

                                          LOUDER TUBA PLAYING

Across town The Duke was infact playing the tuba while
sitting on his thrown. His daughter, THE PRINCESS, is seated
at his side smacking her lips on a piece of chewing gum.
Thier trusy barker Jonah is sitted near by awaiting The
Dukes orders.

                                          PRINCESS CHEWING GUM

                    PRINCESS
                (whiney voice)
            I want to have a party father

                                          CUT TUBA MUSIC

The Duke stops playing tuba momentairily to adress his
council...of ...uh ... well his daughter and Jonah

                    DUKE
            My Daughter is an ideal symbol of,
            beauty, class and wealth, ...If
            it's a party my daughter wants
            ...then it's a party shell
            get....Jonah! ..Draw up a neuvo
            decree!

                    JONAH
            Yes your royal duke....of tubonia.

                    THE PRINCESS
            Yeay... I loooove Parties father

                                          THE PRINCESS CLAPPS

The Princess is pleased and begins claping her hands.

                              RESTART TUBA PLAYING

The Duke resumes playing is staple song on the tube as the
palace buzzez with excitement... meanwhile on the other side
of town...

STEP FATHERS ROOM.

                              STEP FATHER YELLS

                    EVIL STEPFATHER
          COFFEE!

Manderellas wicked Step father screams demanding more Coffee

                    EVIL STEPFATHER
          Coffee... COFFEE!

in the kitchen Manderella races to pour his wicked step
fathers coffee and enters with the extra hot coffee and is
careful not to spill a drop.

                    MANDERELLA
          Here pops..here's your coffee....
          hot just like you like it.

in the distance the faint sound of a Tuba is heard
approaching, three brothers enter the room with the duke and
Jonah.

                    BRO 1
          Holy shit pops you wont believe it,
          this awesome fuckin scroll just
          arrived from the kick ass Duke.

                    BRO 2
          Yeah a scroll pops.

just then Jonah enters the center of the room and drops to
one knees. He clears his throat and clearly announces...

                    JONAH
          Here yee here yee, a party must be
          thrown ....Here ...In the name of
          the princess, by decree of The Duke
          of Tubonia.

confused the brothers hand the scroll down to each other and
over to the eldest brother. the elder brother begins to read
the scroll as The Duke and Jonah exit.

> BRO 3
> Who the fuck is the Duke... and ware the fuck is Tubonia?

> BRO 1
> Who the fuck cares were gonna have a party ...with girls.

> BRO 2
> Yeah ... Tits!

> BRO 1
> There's gonna be a princess at our party, common guys we gotta go get prophylactics.

> BRO 2
> Yeah ... Uh...

> BRO 1
> Condoms....

> BRO 2
> Oh yeah Condoms!

> MANDERELLA
> Can I go too? ...Pops?

all Three brother are horrified at what they just herd and recoil with disgust.

> ALL THREE
> WHAT!... no... no way!

> What are you gonna wear... your smock?

> ALL BROTHERS LAUGH

> MANDERELLA
> I could make something!

> BROTHERS
> Yeah right!... No way!

the wicked step father motions for one of the brothers to come closer... He whispers in one of the brothers ears.

> WHISPERING

                    BRO 3
                (dissapointed)
            Pop's says you can go if you clean
            the whole house... and put some
            clothes on.

                    BRO 2
            Common lets get ready for
            da bitches.

Manderellas brothers exit mocking and making fun of him...
however manderella is so excited for this opportunity their
words don't even phase him this time... Manderella turns to
whisper to himself.

                    MANDERELLA
            I can go?...I can go... I can't
            believe their gonna let me go!

THE ATTIC

Manderella Hurrys up to his room and runs to tell his only
friends... the mice... he looks into the mice bucket and
begins to tell them all about it.

                    MANDEREILA
            I get to go...You here that little
            friends? There's gonna be a party
            with a real princess!
            I got to get to sewing.

Manderella begins to sew. but slowly realizes that It'll
take all day and night to sew a new outfit, and he still has
an entire house to clean...

                    MANDERELLA
            Aww who am I kidding... I'll never
            finish in time, I'll never get the
            dishes done and I still have to sew
            my outfit ....(sighs)maybe... if I
            put my clothes in this trunk and
            pray with all my might maybe a
            miracle will happen!

Manderella Places all of his things into the trunk. He
begins to pray with all his might and then lays back on his
bed and goes to sleep.

                            CUE FGF THEME MUSIC

as soon as Manderella starts to drift away to sleep a
mysterious and fabulos god like Fairy man apears in his
room... this is indeed Mandarellas Fairy God Father(FGF).

Creeping in from the shadows he takes a good look around and then exits Mandarellas room, He heads down to the living room to find Manderellas brothers lifting weights to try and get in shape for the princess... he watches from a distance

LIVING ROOM

                                            WEIGHT LIFTING SOUNDS

occupied by doing curls while eating beef jerky. the middle brother is kissing his biceps flexing in the mirror
            (kissing his bicep)
     Yeah... Kiss it... kiss it

            BRO 2
     Princesses love muscles ...

            BRO 1
     yeah, I've heard that...

all 3 brothers give a nod of agreement and resume lifting weights... The Fairy god father then pulls out a package of sleeping powder, and tip toes up to the brothers three

            BRO 1
     Hay?...who the Fuck is this gu-

                                      TWINKLY HARPSICHORD SOUND

before he can finish his sentence, The Fairy Godfather blows sleeping powder in the face of Manderellas brothers and it goes everywhere. The three brothers quickly become drowsy and nod off. The Fairy Godfather then begins to undress the sleeping brothers.

            FGF
     Giggles These will do just
     dandy ...

Removing items of clothing from each brother The Fairy Godfather giggles with laughter...

                                                  FGF GIGGLING

            FGF
     ...and This too.

The Fairy Godfather then creeps in to the kitchen and speaks the magic words

            FGF
     Pubery, Gooberty, Goo.

                                        MAGICAL CHIMES

and suddenly, as if by Magic, the Kitchen cleans itself and
shimers with a sparkling clean finish.

                                        SPARKLY CLEAN SOUNDS

The Fairy Godfather then tip-toes upstairs to Manderellas
attic room.

THE ATTIC

Up in Manderellas room The Fairy Godfather takes the
clothing he took from Manderellas sleeping brothers and puts
them into the trunk. Into the very same trunk that
Manderella had prayed over... the trunk slams shut
waking Manderella up.

                                        TRUNK LID SLAM

                    MANDERELLA
            What!...huh?...what was that?
            ....The Trunk?

Manderella slowly rises from his bed and crawls over to the
trunk. He raises the lid to look inside

                                        CREEKING TRUNK LID

Astonished at what he sees...Manderella pulls out new
clothing that appears to be a fresly sewen suite with
matching bow tie and golden pair of loafers. He shows them
to the mice his only real friends.

                    MANDERELLA
            Look fellas!... A Miracle! ... a
            real miracle...

Then turning to his fathers crudely made painting

                    MANDERELLA
            Look Dad.... a real miracle!

Manderella stairs deeply...looking at the Painting of his
father as if it were going to reply...

                    MANDEREILA
            oh who am I kidding... you're never
            gonna answer me...

                    FGF
            Ahh ah ahh. I wouldn't say that
            now.

Manderella believes his fathers painting is talking

>   MANDARELLA
>   Dad!?... Is that you... has your
>   spirit come to tell me some
>   fatherly advise?

suddenly his Fairy Godfather places a hand on Manderellas
man-boy shoulder spining him around in his spot looking up
at the strange fairy man Manderella says

>   MANDERELLA
>   Who the fuck are you!?

>   FGF
>   Why I'm your fairy godfather
>   Manderella ...Your father sent
>   me... from beyond the grave ... to
>   watch over you.

Manderellas face lights up with excitement... but then
slowly turns to concern.

>   MANDERELLA
>   Well ... then... where have you
>   been my entire life?... I mean ...I
>   live like shit... Look around.

they both pause and take a slow look around at their
crumbling and pitiful surroundings, to wich Manderellas
Fairy Godfather simply replies

>   FGF
>   Hmm hmm hm That's not important
>   right now... What is important...
>   is that I can perform miracles
>   Manderella.

>   MANDERELLA
>   Miracles?

>   FGF
>   Miracles ...Just close your eyes
>   tight... and repeat after
>   me...Puberty... Gooberty... Goo.

>   MANDERELLA
>   Puberty... ... Gooberty... ... Goo!

                                        FRYING PAN CLANG

All of the sudden the Fairy Godfather bashes manderella up side the head with a frying pan, Knocking Manderella unconcious ...laid out cold The Fairy Godfather begins dressing Manderella in the new clothes

                              CLOTHING RUSTELING

after a few moments of unconciousnes Manderella is awoken in his new cloting all most if by magic... only this time there was no magic, a creepy man undressed and re-dressed manderella while he lay concussed...

                      FGF
           Rise and shine! (Giggles)

                  MANDERELLA
           Wowee! A real Miracle ....thanks
           fairy godfather ......and thanks
           dad...

again talking to the Painting on wall of his father, and as usual with no reply... Manderella then begins to tell his friends the mice...

                  MANDARELLA
           Hey fellas look... a real miracle!

                              CUE VINTAGE PARTY MUSIC

Manderella begins to hear music coming from the party.

                      FGF
           Now hurry along to that princess
           you sweet thing you!

                  MANDERELLA
           Right! I just gotta fix my hair.

LIVING ROOM PARTY

Down in the living room Manderellas three brothers are dancing with other guests

                  BRO 2
           When is the Princess gonna be here?

                  BRO 1
           Uu... I don't know... I don't even
           know what she looks like...

                  BRO 2
           yeah I didn't even know we had a
           princess

both brothers look at their eldest brother and with a blank face he simply shrugs...Just then The Fairy Godfather appears at party. he tip-toes over to a bubble machine that's cranking out bubbles all over the dance floor

                                        BUBBLE MACHINE

un-noticed, The Fairy Godfather puts sleeping glitter into the bubble machine, when sudenly one of the brother notices The Fairy Godfather

> BRO 1
> Hey!... look... It's that...man
> ...lady!

Three brothers look at each other in shock, they begin making their way through the crowd towards The Fairy Godfather. but he begins hands like a magical butterfly and begins to take flight, crowd surfing over the dance party ... just out of reach of Manderellas wicked step brothers

                                        PARTY MUSIC DIPS

THE ATTIC

meanwhile upstiars Manderella is fixing his hair. He takes one last look in the mirror and says to the mice...

> MANDERELLA
> Wish me luck fellas... I'm off to
> meet the princess.

LIVING ROOM PARTY

                                        RESUME PARTY MUSIC

back at the party The Fairy Godfather is surfing the crowd as many sleep-bubbles fill up the air

                                        EVERYONE YAWNING

The circle of people holding up the Fairy Godfather slowly let him down and begin to get very sleepy ... they begin to fall asleep all around him.

                                        FADE IN FGF SONG

everyone including Manderellas wicked step brothers collapse to the floor. the Fairy Godfather rises, twirling around as he steps over the 3 brothers and hides in the closet.

                                        DUKES TUBA MARCH

All of the sudden a Tuba can heard approaching. Manderella enters the seemingly dead party wide eyed.

                    MANDERELLA
          Did I miss the party? ... What's
          going on?...That music!?...

                                    DOOR BREAK WITH GLASS

The Duke and Jonah enter with Tuba blaring and Jonah Drops to one knee

                                          CUT OUT TUBA MARCH

                    JONAH
          Here ye Here ye... Presenting his
          royal duke... ... of Tubonia, And
          his daughter... the Princess.

The Princess enters and Locks eyes Instantly with manderella.

                                              CUE LOVE MUSIC

They immediately fall in love, Manderella runs over to her and She picks him up and twirls him around, just like you imagined she would...

                                        LOVE MUSIC SWELLS

                  MANDERELLA
          I wish you could hold me like this
          forever...

it was a beutiful sight, really it was... time seemed to slow down if only for a moment as she twirl arond all big and fat like a wobbly top, black as the Ace of spades as she were... and Manderella as white as ghost while beaming with tranquility and joy as he clung to princes... well thats how you we're imagining it wern't you... anyways

                                          CELLPHONE RING

just then a cellphone would ring out waking the sleeping guests...

                                        CELLPHONE RINGING

The brothers start to wake up, Manderella knows he will be pummeled for having danced with the princess... he looks deeply into the princesses eyes.

                    MANDERELLA
          I have to go...

                    PRINCESS
          no... but... I don't even know your
          name...

                    MANDERELLA
          Good bye...

Manderellas eldest brother comes to his senses and streaches
out his leg and foot in an attempt to trip Manderella

                                        BODY THUMP AND CRASH

Manderella trips over his eldest brother leaving behind his
glittery goldern loafer. By this time the commotion has
woken up everyone else sleeping on the dance floor. as
Manderella lyes face down palms up on the floor, a small
mouse crawls out of his breast pocket makings a sqeek.

                                        MOUSE SQUEEK

                    JONAH
          A Mouse!

                    THE DUKE
          A mouse?

                    THE PRINCESS
          A Mouse!

                    EVERYONE
          A mouse!!! ahhhhh...

                                        PARTY PANICS

Everyone at the party beings to scream and freaks out. They
all start stampeding towards the door.

                                        STAMPEDE

The Duke of Tubonia begins frantically playing a retreat
song

                                        TUBA RETRETE SONG

The crowd forces Manderella and the princess apart from one
another. Manderella sprints to his attic door in time to
escape his brothers. Whole room is empty except for Jonah
and Princess.

                                        FADE OUT ALL SOUND

  CRICKETS

                    PRINCESS
          MMMMMmmmm ...I like that white boy
          Jonah....

                    JONAH
          He left a shoe.

                                              FADE OUT CRICKETS

PART 3

THE DUKES PLACE

Back at the Dukes palace Manderellas glitter golden loafer
sits on a small pillow. the SHOE BARRER holds the small
pillow and keeps a sharp eye on the pillow, proudly
protecting it for the royal family from any danger. The Duke
sits on his throne scheming

                    DUKE
          He left a shoe aye.......(Rubbing
          hands together)
          ...Jonah!... Another Nuevo
          decree!...
          Everyone in Tubonia must try on
          this glittery golden loafer... the
          man it fits... will go with the
          princess.

Jonah begins scribing as fast as he can, the Shoe Barrer and
The Duke jump up and start marching out the door.

                                                    TUBA MARCH

THE LAND OF TUBONIA

All over the land of Tubonia, The Duke, Jonah, and the Shoe
Barrer marched from house to house stopping at every door
demanding that the all the men in the house try on the
remarkable glittery golden loafer.

RANDOM HOUSE

The first random house they approach has inside a older man
who is watching sports on his couch while smoking a rather
large cigar.

                                              TUBA MARCH APPROACHES

The Duke, Jonah, and the Shoe Barrer kick in the front door
breaking some of the glass in it

DOOR KICK & GLASS BREAK

The older gentleman is surprisingly unphased by the rude entry as he awaits the announcement. Jonah drops to one knee and announces

CUT TUBA MARCH

> JONAH
> Here ye, here ye,... By decree of the Duke... all available men in Tubonia must be fitted with this glittery golden loafer... the man it fits... shall go with the princess...

> OLDER GENTELMEN
> The Hell we will!

just then the older gentelmens young grand son, who has been watching the whole ordeal from his hiding place, reveals himself and addresses the royal precession

> LITTLE BOY
> I wann try the shoe on... I wanna try the shoe on ... I wanna try the shoe on...

> OLDER GENTELMEN
> NO... Stay back Bobby! ....Get the hell outta here before I call the law.

Disapointed, The Duke shrugs and exits the older gentermans home followed by Jonah and the Shoe Barrer

TUBA MARCH

They continue on their quest to find the owner of the glittery golden loafer... unknown by Manderella

RANDOM BATHROOM

meanwhilein a random bathroom across town... a Man sits down on toilet with a newspaper. he thinks nothing of it when he first starts to hear a tuba approaching.

TUBA MARCH

but when his bathroom door is suddenly bashed open and Jonah and the Duke march in with the shoe fitter.

DOOR SMASH OPEN

CUT OUT TUBA MARCH

the random man on the toilet is startled but before he can say anything Jonah drops to one knee and announces...

> JONAH
> Here ye, here ye... by the decree of the Duke everyone in Tubonia must be fitted with this glittery golden loafer.

> GUY ON THE TOILET
> Wait... let me get this straight... You're going around Tubonia, making everyone try on this loafer?...don't you think there's lots of people with the same size shoe?...that's never gonna work ... your gonna need some more definitive evidence like DNA or shoe.... prints....

The Duke looks at Jonah, who looks at the Shoe Barrer... who looks completely lost. For the first time all three men realize their efforts might be completely in vain... could their really be more then one person in Tubonia that this shoe could fit? Convinced the man on the toilet must be crazy the royal family shake it off and exit the mans bathroom continuing on their quest

TUBA MARCH

> GUY ON THE TOILET
> Hay? who's gonna fix this door now?

unphased by the citizens request The Duke, Jonah and the Shoe Barrer march on... mean while back at Manderellas house his step father listens to complaints from his wicked step brothers

STEP FATHERS ROOM

> BRO 1
> Manderella ruined everything pops, you gonna let him go un-punished like that?!

> BRO 2
> Yeah he's gotta be punished!

> MANDERELLA
> I didn't try to ruin anythin--

BRO 1
          Shut up!

                    BRO 2
          Yeah...Shut!... Up!

                    BRO 1
          Wait... you guy's hear that?

Everyone quiets down.

                              (FAINT TUBA MARCH)

                              TUBA MARCH SWELLS

The step Father raises his hand with a key in it. All three
brothers flash a wicked grin at each other as they take the
key from their father and plan to lock Manderella in the
attic with it.

                              BROTHERS LAUGHING

Manderella tries to run for it

                              FOOTSTEPS THEN STRUGGLE

but it's no use... Manderellas brothes are bigger and
stronger then him... they easily subdue him and drag him to
his attic room locking the door

                              CUT OUT STRUGGLE

                              DOOR LOCK SOUND

                    MANDEREILA
          Comon fellas... this aint fair...

                              BANGING ON THE DOOR

                    MANDEREILA
          you can't do this to me...

                    BROTHERS
          SHUT UP!

                    BRO 1
          I swear if you make a peep were
          gonna feed you to the raccoons!

Manderellas brothers return to living room to prepare for
The Dukes arrival... Leaving Manderella hiddin in the attic
with no way to get out...

THE ATTIC

devastated by his brothers actions he begins to hear The Duke and the Royal Shoe Precession approacing

>   TUBA MARCH SWELLS

Manderella begins to go mad... that shoe is his shoe... it was given to him from his Fairy Godfather... who came to him by way of his very own father from beyond the grave... Manderella was always a bit dramtic and in an attempt to take his own life he slowly raises a big rambo knife to his throat as if to cut his own head off when he is suddenly intrupted by his Fairy Godfather

> FGF
> Nu uhhhh uhhh!... Wait unitl your marriage fails and you get a divorce before you do that.

startled manderella drops the knife from this throat... His Fairy Godfather flashes a friendly smile and presents manderella with a spare key to the attic door.

> MANDERELLA
> Its another miracle!

Grinning with joy they both begin to hatch a plan... downstairs however The Duke has arrived with the shoe and is about to enter and make his announcment

THE LIVING ROOM

>   TUBA MARCH SWELL
>
>   DOOR SMASH AND GLASS
>
>   CUT OUT TUBA

> JONAH
> Here ye, here ye... by decree of this royal Duke of Tubonia... all men in the land shall try on this glittery golden loafer... the man it fits... shall go with the princess

> BRO 1
> Wait...why that looks like my shoe... yea thats my shoe let me go first!

                    BRO 2
          Like hell it is... that's my shoe

both brothers stop and look at their eldest brother who
shakes his head in disapproval... the two other wicked step
brothers back off and let their eldest brother sit in the
chair first... he begins to struggle to put the shoe on, and
forces his fat foot in the shoe making bulge all around and
appear as if hes attempting to bake bread in his shoes...

                    BRO 1
          wow ... look... it uh... fits...
          like a glove

                    BRO 2
          yea it certainly ... looks like it

Just then Manderella barges in and startling the entire room

                    MANDEREILA
          wait... stop... that's my shoe...
          and I'm the man-boy who's gonna go
          with the princess...

the brothers try to play if off as if its a complete joke in
fact they start laughing at him

                              BROTHERS LAUGHING

not distracted by the laughing Jonah's keen eye spots the
other mate to the glittery golden loafer on Manderellas
other foot...

                    JONAH
          My lord!.... Look

Jonah points out the shoe to The Duke... The Duke stares in
amazement and knows from the the very sight of his one shoed
feet... this is indeed the man-boy who will go with the
princess... The Duke breaths in a giant breath and gives a
hard blow upon his mighty tuba....

                              TUBA WEDDING SONG

THE WEDDING
              (long beat)

                              WEDDNG SONG DIP

and so it would be written that Manderella was to go with
the princess and on her wedding day everyone in Tubonia
showed up... the random strangers from around town... the
crude painting o this father gave Manderella away in fact

... even his wicked step family... as the cerimony opened everyone commenced to clapping as Jonah married the two before everyone in Tubonia

                    JONAH
do you Uh ... Mandarella... take the princess to be you Lawfully wedded wife?

                    MANDEREILA
Do I?... Yes... yes of course I do...

                    JONAH
And do you Princess... take this uh... man-boy to be your lawfully wedded man-boy?

                    PRINCESS
I dew!

                    JONAH
then by the power invested in me by The Duke Of Tubonias decree... I now declare you .... man-boy and wife... you may kiss the bride!

                                      KISS

                            CHEERING AND CLAPPING

                                HELILUJAH SONG

                        ALL CAST CLAPS AND SINGS

                  ALL CAST
helilujah... ...halilujah, halilujah... it's a mericle!

helilujah... ...halilujah, halilujah... it's a mericle!

helilujah... ...halilujah, halilujah... it's a mericle!

                                WEDDING SOUNDS DIP

                  NARRATOR
so thats the story of Manderella and how a simple man boy servent would grow up to find true love even though he grew up in a shitty house on the poor side of town.

FADE OUT ALL SOUND

THE GARBAGE ALLEY

FADE IN CITY SOUNDS

                NARRATOR
so now... where Manderellas once crumbly house stood is nothing more then a garbage alley... they say is you listen late at night you can still hear the sound of Manderella throwing balogna into the wind...

                MANDERELLA
hay!... you guys make sure you share some of that bologna with the raccoons... I don't wanna see em scracthin around the palace ya hear?

                BRO 1
Yes sir...

                BRO 2
whatever you say manderella

                NARRATOR
so there you have it... I hope you learned something from our very fairy tale... farewell to you... and our mandarella

FADE IN OUTRO MUSIC

-The End-

RADIO CREDITS

CREDITS

Manderella was written by Milton Horowitz for The Cleveland Radio Players. Radio play recorded at Bad Racket Studios. Published by The Cleveland Radio Player

to learn more about how to purchase rights/roalties and additional scripts please visit

www.clevelandradioplayers.com

Rights and Royalties

Originally adapted for the radio and performed by The Cleveland Radio Players

Directed by Milton Matthew Horowitz

Recorded at Bad Racket Studios

For more information on performance rights and royalties, or to listen to Manderella as a radio play, please visit www.ClevelandRadioPlayers.com

www.ingramcontent.com/pod-product-compliance
Lightning Source LLC
Chambersburg PA
CBHW081025040426
42444CB00014B/3353